The Bible's languag[...] full, wide, and consis[...] never be explained a[...] exploration of an id[...] beginning, Dr. Jones [...] as a step beyond accuracy. He has shown us the way to love what we may have once feared.

Mark A. Garcia,
Pastor, Immanuel Orthodox Presbyterian Church & President and
Lecturer in Scripture and Theology, Greystone Theological Institute,
Coraopolis, Pennsylvania

When the church discovers that it is systematically neglecting or obscuring large New Testament themes, there seem to be three possible responses: ignorance and inertia; radicalism and revolution; or reformation and renewal. In this vital little book, Mark Jones has chosen the third approach, providing us with a timely application of Scripture and the Reformed tradition. I know myself and other Christians around me need all the motivation Scripture has to offer, and I'm grateful that Dr. Jones is on the case to help us reconsider God's promises to reward our good works done in Christ and the Spirit. This is a wise and careful work. Those who put in a little work and have ears to hear will be richly rewarded.

Jason B. Hood,
Director of Advanced Urban Ministerial Education, Gordon Conwell
Theological Seminary, Hamilton, Massachusetts

Mark Jones shows with theological balance, biblical clarity, and pastoral sensitivity why it is our highest honor to imitate God as his dear children, and why it is our greatest joy for him to reward our works by his mercies in Christ. This book fills a great need in the church today and offers hope to those who wish to love the Savior who first loved them.

Ryan McGraw,
Professor of Systematic Theology, Greenville Presbyterian
Theological Seminary

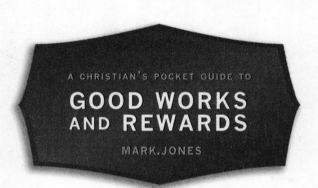

A CHRISTIAN'S POCKET GUIDE TO

GOOD WORKS
AND REWARDS

MARK.JONES

In this Life and the Next

paperback ISBN 978-1-5271-0044-2
epub ISBN 978-1-5271-0071-8
mobi ISBN 978-1-5271-0072-5

10 9 8 7 6 5 4 3 2 1

Printed in 2017
Published by Christian Focus Publications Ltd,
Geanies House, Fearn, Ross-shire,
IV20 1TW, Scotland, Great Britain
www.christianfocus.com

Cover design by Daniel Van Straaten
Printed and bound by Nørhaven, Denmark.

Dedicated to Selwyn Vandeyar
(Matthew 6:33)

CONTENTS

⚠ Warning
🖉 Don't Forget
⑦ Stop and Think
✴ Point of Interest

INTRODUCTION

Many Bible passages speak of God rewarding his people while many others call such redeemed individuals sinners. When you consider who we are by nature (sinners), and who God is in his nature (holy, righteous, just), it seems a little presumptuous—perhaps even delusional?—to speak of God 'rewarding' us. Jesus came to save sinners, but does he reward such people for their works? Impossible! Or, if it is true, maybe it would be best not to discuss it too much. Hence the shortage of books on the topics of good works and rewards.

In North American circles especially, I have noticed that Christians (even pastors) tend to be squeamish about the topic of rewards. There are likely many reasons for this phenomenon, such as the fear of appearing Roman Catholic, legalistic, or self-dependent. But I want to put forward a positive case for stressing both the importance and value of the doctrine of rewards for the Christian life. In one respect, the doctrine of rewards glorifies the Father, Son, and Holy Spirit in unique ways and also blesses our neighbors. Also, the Bible frequently highlights God rewarding his people. This usually takes place to motivate believers to necessary good works and deter them from neglecting fruits of repentance.

Good works are not an option for Christians. But at the same time, they are not to be done simply because they are obligatory. Good works are done for many reasons, such as gratefulness for what God has done for us. One less obvious reason concerns what I call 'holy self–interest'—the desire to be rewarded by God.

The potential abuse and pastoral problems attached to this doctrine do not nullify its legitimate use and the necessity to discuss it. Many misuse the doctrine of justification by faith alone, but Protestant theologians were not deterred from boldly proclaiming it as the free and gracious right to eternal life through faith alone. Glorious doctrines, such as this or the incarnation, are often misunderstood, which in part makes them so magnificent. Many truths of the Christian faith make no sense to the world and even confuse Christians. Remember the disciples' failure to understand the imminent death and resurrection of Christ? The apparent absurdity of certain teachings often highlights their inexpressible majesty and exclusive origin—these are truths from a God who exists above and beyond us.

Hopefully those reluctant to discuss good works and rewards will give this book a sympathetic and fair reading. By all means, put the Scriptural evidence that

I present for this doctrine to the 'Berean' test. My hope and confident expectation is that you will see the grace of God stamped all over this doctrine and be motivated to love him and your neighbor like never before.

'Therefore, my beloved brothers, be steadfast, immovable, always abounding in the work of the Lord, knowing that in the Lord your labor is not in vain' (1 Cor. 15:58). Amen. The work of God's servants are never in vain: 'For God is not unjust so as to overlook your work and the love that you have shown for his name in serving the saints, as you still do' (Heb. 6:10).

The Teaching of Protestant Ministers

I am sure I have heard as many of our ministers preach as he, and read as many of their books as he, yet I can testify that I never heard or read them opposing 'the Christian doctrine of good works.' Often I have heard and found them pressing a universal obedience to the whole law of God; teaching men to abound in good works; pressing the indispensable necessity of them from the commands of law and gospel; encouraging men unto them by the blessed promises of acceptance and reward in Christ; declaring them to be the way of men's coming to the kingdom of heaven; affirming that all that believe are created in Christ Jesus unto good works, and for men to neglect, to despise them, is wilfully to neglect their own salvation. But 'opposing the Christian doctrine of good works,' and that with 'sayings culled out of St Paul's Epistle to the Romans,' I never heard, I never read, any Protestant minister…If he intend that, God having graciously promised to accept and receive them in Christ, they become thereupon acceptable and rewardable, —this, Protestant ministers teach daily. – John Owen[1]

1

IF GOD IS FOR US

God is not just a good God; he is goodness. He is infinitely good. All that he does is good, lest his goodness be called into question. What we do reflects who we are (Matt. 12:35). For God this is especially true.

As Christians, we see God's goodness principally in Christ. In light of such goodness to us in his Son, we must learn his ways, because they are good, as are his commandments. We say with the Psalmist, 'You are good and do good; teach me your statutes' (Ps. 119:68).

We aim to do good because we are children of a good God. We must not 'grow weary of doing good' (Gal. 6:9). Our Lord understood, as the Son of God, that he had an obligation to imitate his heavenly Father. Thus Christ went about doing good (Acts 10:38), even in the greatest suffering (Luke 23:34), leaving us a pattern and example (1 Pet. 2:20–21). God's children are to reflect him in all of his moral attributes (holiness, goodness, wisdom, justice, truth, etc.).

If we refuse to do good or claim we cannot, we fail to properly understand God's goodness to us in Christ, which includes sending the Spirit into our hearts to make us good. Our Christian witness is built on both our message and our deeds. Paul implores Titus: 'Show yourself in all respects to be a model of good works' (Titus 2:7). Our light must shine before men (Matt. 5:16).

God is for us as he makes us like him in his moral excellence and overcomes our defacement by sin. As Christians, we are to 'put on the new self, created to be like God in true righteousness and holiness' (Eph. 4:24). His grace towards us makes us good: 'The good person out of his good treasure brings forth good' (Matt. 12:35). God does not stop with his Son, the perfect image of goodness, but shares his glory with those who belong to him. Such glory includes our conformity to his image (Rom. 8:29).

MERCIFUL AND GRACIOUS

If we grant that God makes us good through his redemptive power in Christ, we then can ask, 'Can God possibly *reward* his people for their good works?' To answer that question, we need to understand the grace of God. Our opinions on whether he rewards good works are, in many respects, tied closely to our view of God.

We may, perhaps unwittingly, be calling into question an aspect of his being when we affirm or deny certain things about him.

God is merciful and gracious: 'But you, O Lord, are a God merciful and gracious, slow to anger and abounding in steadfast love and faithfulness' (Ps. 86:15; see also Ps. 103:8). Again,

> The LORD is gracious and merciful,
>   slow to anger and abounding in steadfast love.
> The LORD is good to all,
>   and his mercy is over all that he has made. (Ps. 145:8)

The grace of God refers to his favor towards his creatures, particularly when they are undeserving of it. Grace is free, unmerited favor. If Adam received grace, then believers post–Fall obtain even greater grace. The grace Adam received did not have its basis in the mercy of the redemptive work of Christ, which is a crucial difference between pre and post–Fall grace.

God relates to all creatures to some degree in grace (Matt. 5:44–45; Ps. 36:5–6), as he gives gifts to all his creatures. The grace that is offered to the church, however, is a 'super–abounding' grace because it leads to eternal life. Quite apart from the glories of God's grace mentioned in Ephesians 1, the chapters that follow provide an extended commentary on his grace towards the church. For example, in chapter two, the God who is 'rich in mercy' (Eph. 2:4) has 'great love' towards us as the spiritually dead made alive in Christ (v. 5). This serves to 'show the immeasurable riches of his grace and kindness toward us in Christ Jesus' (v. 7). We are saved 'by grace' or the 'gift of God,' totally apart from our own doing (v. 8). This gift includes good works that he prepared 'beforehand, that we should walk in them' (v. 10). The question certainly arises, 'How can God reward his faithful servants for good works he works in us?' (Eph. 2:10). This question can only be answered when we consider it in light of God's grace.

Whatever we receive must come from our Heavenly Father above (John 3:27; James 1:17), which ought to humble us. We find no stingy God in the Scriptures who keeps the heavens shut and refuses to bless his people. No, if he will 'tear open' the heavens and send his Son to die for our sins, 'how will he not also with him graciously give us all things?' (Rom. 8:32).

 Since grace is unmerited favor, we understand that Adam received grace from God before the fall. What is the difference between the grace that Adam received before the fall and the grace that believers receive now after the fall?

IN THE BEGINNING

When God created Adam and Eve to rule the garden, which was a temple where mankind uniquely enjoyed God's presence, he gave them tasks. As a prophet, priest, and king, God commanded Adam to 'work' and 'keep' the garden (Gen. 2:15) as part of his duty to subdue the earth (Gen. 1:28). As image-bearers of God, Adam and Eve functioned as vice-regents on earth, which needed more 'filling' of people who were children of God, to the glory of his name.

Many theologians have argued that God would have rewarded Adam for his personal and perfect obedience. There has been some dispute over what the reward would have been, but many have said that Adam and Eve, upon passing a period of probation, would have entered into some sort of 'heavenly' existence in which they were incapable of sin and could eat from the tree of life and live forever (Gen. 3:22). In other words, there was always the promise of reward for faithful work. Such is based upon the context of 'covenant' whereby God speaks of promises and threats. As Thomas Watson says, without being overly dogmatic, 'In case man had stood, it is probable he would not have died, but would have been translated to a better paradise.'[2]

God's pattern of creation is one of work and rest, not only for him but also his creatures. Subsequent biblical revelation shows that the creation pattern remains, without abrogation, the blueprint for the redemptive pattern. The rest for which we strive is ultimately heavenly (Heb. 3–4). God gives to us, through Christ, what was originally held out to Adam as a reward for his work. We enter God's rest through Christ, the second Adam.

The reward likely offered to Adam for his faithfulness went beyond what he could have earned, which highlights the grace of God in his covenantal dealings with Adam and Eve. Adam depended totally upon God, and required his assistance, through the Holy Spirit, to offer up acceptable obedience to his Father. Self-dependence would have been a sin against God, and self-dependence, in the form of unbelief, actually led Adam and Eve into sin. They should have depended upon the Holy Spirit to believe the words of warning spoken by their Father.

Adam could never say that God owed him anything, for, as Christ said, 'when you have done all that you were commanded, say, "We are unworthy servants; we have only done what was our duty"' (Luke 17:10). Yet, according to the terms of the covenant, God would have rewarded Adam for his obedience in a manner that far exceeded its worth. In this way, we see God acting in grace because he granted an undeserved reward. This remains the case even in a context of a 'works' relationship. Just as the covenant with Adam has rightly been called a 'covenant of works,' it is also appropriately known as a 'covenant of life' and a 'covenant of friendship with God.' All are fitting phrases.

ALL HAVE TURNED ASIDE

Sin entered the world through Adam's rebellion against a gracious God. As God's vice-regent on earth, with a unique calling as a 'king,' and being the son of God, Adam's sin had deleterious consequences for all of his posterity. As David borrows richly the biblical vocabulary on sin, he makes an important point: our fundamental problem is not what we do, but who we are. We are 'brought forth in iniquity' and conceived in sin (Ps. 51:5). In other words, at the moment of conception, we stand guilty and polluted before a holy, righteous God. Adam's transgression rendered us obnoxious to God.

The Bible calls us sinners, but does not stop at such in describing what we are. While we are often tempted to downplay our natural wickedness, the Scriptures give us a picture of what a real sinner looks like (Rom. 3:12–18):

> 'All have turned aside; together they have become worthless;
>> no one does good,
>> not even one.
> 'Their throat is an open grave;
>> they use their tongues to deceive.
> 'The venom of asps is under their lips.
> 'Their mouth is full of curses and bitterness.
> 'Their feet are swift to shed blood;
>> in their paths are ruin and misery,
>> and the way of peace they have not known.
> 'There is no fear of God before their eyes.'

Paul's description of humankind does not flatter. One will not see such a personal description on a dating site. But this section in Romans 3 tells the truth about all of us apart from grace. For example, no one does good, 'not even one.' We are guilty before God because all our actions proceed from the flesh without the principle of faith and love.

That we could do a good work 'in the flesh'—such as believe the gospel or worship acceptably—is foreign to the teaching of God's word. We are morally bankrupt before God and deserve his wrath and damnation. Talk of pleasing him, or being rewarded by him, remains utterly foolish for those under his wrath (Eph. 2:1).

Oddly, however, some Christians seem to take this truth and import it into the Christian life. Just as it is wrong to consider ourselves 'too good' before we are converted, it is also wrong for us to consider ourselves 'too bad' after we have been converted. This gets to the heart of this book on rewards. Who is God? And who are we, in Christ? These are the two fundamental questions we need to answer to know whether God will reward Christians for their good works.

 Why is it wrong to consider ourselves 'too bad' after we have been converted? What are some ways that we do this?

2

THE TRINITARIAN BASIS FOR REWARDS

When we are brought into the family of God, through faith, by the power of the Holy Spirit, in the name of Christ, our relationship to God changes. In Eden, God was Adam's Father as well as his God: 'the son of Adam, the son of God' (Luke 3:38). Redeemed Israel were also children of God (Deut. 32:6):

> Do you thus repay the LORD,
>   you foolish and senseless people?
> Is not he your father, who created you,
>   who made you and established you?

Or, Isaiah 64:8,

'But now, O LORD, you are our Father;
    we are the clay, and you are our potter;
    we are all the work of your hand.'

In the New Covenant, sonship does not change, but it is brought into clearer light. We are sons of God through our Lord Jesus Christ. In union with Jesus Christ, we share in his own identity. He is the Son of God; we are sons of God. He pours forth his Spirit into our hearts, 'by whom we cry, "Abba! Father!"' The Spirit himself bears witness with our spirit that we are children of God' (Rom. 8:15–16). In his classic work *Knowing God*, J.I. Packer calls adoption the 'highest privilege that the gospel offers.'[3] He adds:

> In adoption, God takes us into his family and fellowship—he establishes us as his children and heirs. Closeness, affection and generosity are at the heart of the relationship. To be right with God the Judge [i.e., justification] is a great thing, but to be loved and cared for by God the Father [i.e., adoption] is a greater.[4]

The reality that God is our Father becomes crucial for understanding whether he will reward our good works or not. Even the statement, 'God is our Father,' ought to settle the matter. Parents understand the joy that obedient children bring, even if their compliance falls short of the perfection rendered by Christ. God is no hard taskmaster, reaping where he has not sown (Matt. 25:24). He remembers we are dust (Ps. 103:14) and treats us accordingly.

As our Father, he accepts less than absolute perfection only because Jesus provided it in our place. Moreover, our works are now pleasing to God because we (as persons) are pleasing to him as a result of our unshakable new identity in Christ. We have a 'person–work' order in our Christian life.

Returning to the concept of parents and their children, consider the artwork of our small children. At different times, fathers receive pictures created by their children. Maybe it is a crayon drawing filled with unpolished scribbles and stick figures. To most, the picture elicits no response, but fathers react with pleasure. They are simply delighted to receive the heartfelt efforts of their children because they are, after all, *their* children. The son or daughter doing the drawing provides the greatest reason for why their 'artwork' pleases the father. In like manner, God accepts the 'sincere obedience' and work of his children. *The Westminster Confession of Faith* sets forth a delightful subsection in chapter 16 on this principle:

> Yet notwithstanding, the persons of believers being accepted through Christ, their good works also are accepted in him, not as though they were in this life wholly unblamable and unreprovable in God's sight; but that he, looking upon them in his Son, is pleased to accept and reward that which is sincere, although accompanied with many weaknesses and imperfections.

God does not look upon us 'in the flesh,' but he looks upon us in the one who became flesh, Jesus Christ the Son of God. God is our Father: 'Every perfect gift is from above, coming down from the Father of lights, with whom there is no variation or shadow due to change' (James 1:17). All the blessings we receive as Christians, we receive as children of our Father in heaven.

 How do you think of yourself? How does the truth that God is your Father affect the way you think of yourself?

Our Christian conduct flows out of our understanding of who we are. For example, in the Sermon on the Mount, Jesus commands his disciples to love their enemies: 'Love your enemies and pray for those who persecute you, so that you may be sons of your Father who is in heaven' (Matt. 5:44–45). We can identify sons of God by the fact that they love their enemies just as the Son of God loved his enemies. His identity as God's son necessitated and guaranteed such love. God rewarded him for such faithful and demanding conduct, and he will reward you too.

Christ makes this clear a little later in the Sermon on the Mount. In chapter 6, we read of the danger of practicing our righteousness before others in order to be seen by them (Matt. 6:1). Christ warns of those who have received their earthly and empty 'reward', but forfeit that which is heavenly and genuine from their Father (Matt. 6:2). Hence, Christian giving should ordinarily be done in secret with 'your left hand not knowing what your right hand is doing.' The result? 'Your Father who sees in secret will reward you' (Matt. 6:4). Matthew Henry, in his commentary on this passage, observes, 'He will reward thee; not as a master who gives his servant what he earns, and no more, but as a Father who gives abundantly to his son that serves him.'[5]

We rob God of his identity as a gracious Father when we deny ourselves what he clearly and graciously promises. So, it is not wrong to ask, 'Does God reward Christians for their good works?' But we would do better to inquire, 'Does our heavenly Father, out of his abundant grace, reward his children for their good works?'

I AM GLORIFIED IN THEM

The good works that Christians perform are always in the name of Christ: 'And whatever you do, in word or deed, do everything in the name of the Lord Jesus, giving thanks to God the Father through him' (Col. 3:17). Our good works relate to his glory. But in discussing his glory, we should know that the Lord Jesus possesses three distinct but interrelated glories.

First, as very God of very God, he is the God of glory (Acts 7:2). Each person in the blessed Trinity is co-equal in glory and majesty. All sharing equally in the divine essence, the three persons possess an infinite and unchangeable glory that they alone can fully understand, see, and enjoy. It is a glory utterly beyond what we can comprehend. As Christians, we can ascribe to God praise and glory (1 Chron. 16:29). Technically, this adds nothing to God's glory, yet our praise, worship, and obedience are still understood as 'glorifying God.'

The triune God's infinite glory remains too high, illustrious, and marvellous for us to understand. It is utterly beyond our powers, and even a small drop of his glory, so to speak, would utterly consume us. With the entrance of sin into the world, this reality becomes even more pronounced (see Exod. 33:20).

Second, we behold the glory of God in the person of Jesus Christ (2 Cor. 3:18; 4:6), not only in this life, but also in the life to come. Jesus possesses a peculiar glory unique to him. The Father and the Spirit do not share this specific glory, for they are not fully God and fully man in their divinity. Christ alone exists as the God-man (*theanthropos*), a 'complex person' or 'composite person' according to theologians. Thus he owns a distinct glory, also called a 'personal glory.'

As a result of the incarnation, there exists a magnificent display of God's glory in the person of Christ. God could display his glory by making millions of worlds, but even these would not compare to the glory that we behold in the person of Christ. After all, he is the visible image of the invisible God (Col. 1:15). That cannot be said of any other person, much less millions of created worlds all furnished with glories.

Third, Christ possesses a mediatorial glory. As a result of his work on behalf of his people, Christ purchased a glory not only for himself but also for his bride. He cannot be content to receive glory for himself, but desires that his bride also share his glory. Since we cannot have his essential divine or personal glory as the God-man, we are left sharing in the glory he purchased for our sake.

We may call this a 'superadded glory.' This involves Christ's people, because they are, after all, his bride.

And the bride of Christ possesses his glory, just as a woman expresses the glory of man (1 Cor. 11:7). We, who are his body, are 'the fullness of him who fills all in all' (Eph. 1:23).

Jesus delights to share his glory with his bride, the church. How does this truth affect the way we view the church and our place in it?

As the bride of Christ obtains the blessings of his work on their behalf, he thereby receives glory. He sees the fruit of his labor. The more blessings Christ pours out from heaven as the resurrected king of glory, the more he gets glory. In fact, the more love Christ shows to the church, the more he shows to himself. For, the man who loves his wife, loves himself (Eph. 5:28). Thus, in his bride, Christ is glorified: 'As for Titus, he is my partner and fellow worker for your benefit. And as for our brothers, they are messengers of the churches, the glory of Christ' (2 Cor. 8:23). 'All mine are yours, and yours are mine, and I am glorified in them' (John 17:10).

Since God's great end concerns the glory of his Son (Col. 1:16), he must be glorified in those for whom he died. He makes the church pure, beautiful, and holy. Spouses all desire (at least they should) to improve their spouse. But most of the time we fail, because we lack the power to do so. But Christ is not in such a position. He not only has the power to make us beautiful, but he remains willing to do so.

Our good works are done only because Christ lived

and died to make them possible. Peter declares, 'He himself bore our sins in his body on the tree, that we might die to sin and live to righteousness. By his wounds you have been healed' (1 Pet. 2:24). In other words, Christ died so we could and would do good works. His death will not be in vain. For God to reward our good works, then, expresses his pleasure with the work of his Son.

If we think about God rewarding our good works in terms of his honoring his Son's work, perhaps we will be less nervous about this topic. It is wonderful to think of God honoring and rewarding his Son by rewarding us for our good works done in Christ's name. This keeps us from being too anthropocentric about rewards and places a more Christ–centered focus on our approach to this important doctrine. Perhaps those who have spoken about good works have missed this particular focus on God honoring his Son through us. Whatever the case, failure to mention this point botches the explanation of the glory of this doctrine.

YOU ARE NOT IN THE FLESH BUT IN THE SPIRIT

The Westminster Confession of Faith highlights the ability of Christians to do good works 'not at all of themselves, but wholly from the Spirit of Christ' (WCF 16.3). This leads not to inactivity, but activity. Such good works, however, cannot emerge from our strength alone. The power comes from God, though the acts remain truly ours.

The presence of the Holy Spirit in us, as he enables us to do good works, plays an important role in whether

God accepts and rewards the good works of believers. The Spirit enables us to do good works in accordance with the commandments of God. We do not simply obey 'externally' but also 'internally' due to a changed heart. Thus, the root of love must be present in all of our good works. Otherwise, they fail to be good.

The fruit of the Spirit is love. To possess him entails possessing love. We therefore obey as loving creatures with hearts changed by the Spirit of Christ. In light of this, one fundamental point needs to be clearly made: God accepts and rewards our works not because of any intrinsic merit in ourselves, but because our good works are performed by the power of the Holy Spirit. As a result, for God to reject our good Spirit-wrought deeds, he would not only be rejecting us, but also himself. In summary, God not only looks upon our good works in Christ, but also in the Spirit. As Ezekiel says on behalf of the Lord (Ezek. 36:26–30):

> And I will give you a new heart, and a new spirit I will put within you. And I will remove the heart of stone from your flesh and give you a heart of flesh. And I will put my Spirit within you, and cause you to walk in my statutes and be careful to obey my rules. You shall dwell in the land that I gave to your fathers, and you shall be my people, and I will be your God. And I will deliver you from all your uncleannesses. And I will summon the grain and make it abundant and lay no famine upon you. I will make the fruit of the tree and the increase of the field abundant, that you may never again suffer the disgrace of famine among the nations.

God promises a 'new heart' and a 'new spirit' in his people so that they can walk according to his commandments. He undertakes to do for them what they cannot in themselves. It would be exceedingly odd, then, for God to reject their obedience in light of the promises he made to his people. But to show his exceeding grace towards sinners, he even promises to reward them with temporal blessings (vv. 29–30).

As those in the Spirit, we belong to Christ, who also abides in us through the Spirit (Rom. 8:9–10). Our identity has changed, and the principle of our actions has been radically altered. From being unable to please God (Rom. 8:8), we now can (1 Thess. 2:4) as 'the aroma of Christ to God among those who are being saved' (2 Cor. 2:15).

3

WHAT CONSTITUTES GOOD WORKS?

If we are serious about wishing to be rewarded for good works, we first need to understand what God deems good works. We may think something is a good work, but if God has not commanded it then we cannot be confident that it will be rewarded. As we read in *The Westminster Confession of Faith* (16:1–2), 'Good works are only such as God has commanded in His holy Word…These good works, done in obedience to God's commandments, are the fruits and evidences of a true and lively faith.'

God alone determines what constitutes a good work. If he accepts and rewards good works, then he must determine what qualifies as a good work. Very simply, for Christians in the New Covenant, the Ten Commandments (Exod. 20:1–17) provide a guide for what constitutes a good work. This occurs in all of the wide-ranging applications of these commandments, including the positive side of each. The Ten Commandments are all reaffirmed in the New Testament. 1 Timothy 1:8–11, for example, gives us what might be most of the Decalogue:

> [8] Now we know that the law is good, if one uses it lawfully, [9] understanding this, that the law is not laid down for the just but for the lawless and disobedient, for the ungodly and sinners, for the unholy and profane, for those who strike their fathers and mothers, for murderers, [10] the sexually immoral, men who practice homosexuality, enslavers, liars, perjurers, and whatever else is contrary to sound doctrine, [11] in accordance with the gospel of the glory of the blessed God with which I have been entrusted.

Note, then:

> 5th commandment = v. 9 'those who strike their fathers and mothers'
> 6th commandment = v. 9 'murderers'
> 7th commandment = v. 10 'the sexual immoral'
> 8th commandment = v. 10 'enslavers'
> 9th commandment = v. 10 'liars, perjurers'

Elsewhere in the New Testament, Paul writes commands to Christian believers that are identical to the form of words first delivered by Moses to the Israelites. Of course, he sometimes speaks generally of the application of God's law: 'For the whole law is fulfilled in one word: "You shall love your neighbor as yourself"' (Gal. 5:14). However, Romans 13:8–10 gives the Decalogue form:

Owe no one anything, except to love each other, for the one who loves another has fulfilled the law. For the commandments, 'You shall not commit adultery, You shall not murder, You shall not steal, You shall not covet,' and any other commandment, are summed up in this word: 'You shall love your neighbor as yourself.' Love does no wrong to a neighbor; therefore love is the fulfilling of the law.

And also in Ephesians 6:2–3, '"Honor your father and mother" (this is the first commandment with a promise), "that it may go well with you and that you may live long in the land."' Note the actual wording 'that it may go well...' comes directly from the Decalogue.

God's requirements are not more than the Ten Commandments, but they are not less either. The commandments must not, however, be viewed too narrowly. For instance, in Ephesians 4, Paul shows what God actually requires in his commandments:

[25] Therefore, having put away falsehood, let each one of you speak the truth with his neighbor, for we are members one of another...[28] Let the thief no longer steal, but rather let him labor, doing honest work with his own hands, so that he may have something to share with anyone in need. [29] Let no corrupting talk come out of your mouths, but only such as is good for building up, as fits the occasion, that it may give grace to those who hear.'

Whatever is forbidden ('having put away falsehood'), the opposite is commanded ('speak the truth'). For example, the eighth commandment forbids stealing, but it also commands generosity. The ninth commandment not only forbids lying, but commands telling the truth.

 The Ten Commandments encompass more than just the bare commands. Think about how the fact that the commandments include positive and negative aspects should impact how you view Christian living.

MAKE THE TREE GOOD AND ITS FRUIT GOOD

As noted above, our Father in heaven bestows upon us names, titles, and descriptions out of pure grace. Christians, by virtue of their union with Christ and all that such signifies (e.g. possessing the Holy Spirit), are described as pure in heart, righteous, and good. Only the good can perform good works. Thus, Christ says that a tree is known by its fruit. What is spoken by a person reflects their heart (Matt. 12:35–37):

> The good person out of his good treasure brings forth good, and the evil person out of his evil treasure brings forth evil. I tell you, on the day of judgment people will give account for every careless word they speak, for by your words you will be justified, and by your words you will be condemned.

Those in the flesh cannot please God; they are evil. The person determines the work: a bad person performs bad works; a good person performs good works. Christ says so explicitly: 'The good person out of his good treasure brings forth good' (Matt. 12:35).

This has great practical relevance to our Christian

ethics. Do we command people to be good if they are bad? Before people can be good, they must first repent and receive forgiveness. They need acceptance with God through Christ; they need to receive the Holy Spirit. They need God to make them good before they can begin to think about being good. But once God deals graciously with a person and fills them with himself, the Scriptures are clear that such a person is good. They must therefore live in accordance with who they are. Out of the abundance of the heart, we shall speak and act.

WITHOUT FAITH
IT IS IMPOSSIBLE TO PLEASE HIM

Additionally, a good work must be done by faith. The Christian life begins, continues, and ends with faith. We live by faith in the Son of God (Gal. 2:20). Indeed, 'without faith it is impossible to please him, for whoever would draw near to God must believe that he exists and that he rewards those who seek him' (Heb. 11:6).

God is pleased by our actions in faith. As we, by faith, draw near to him, believing that he exists, we do so with the confident hope that he will reward us. True faith never goes unrewarded, because God has promised rewards for acts of faith.

Hebrews 11 presents Moses as one who lived by faith. He kept the first commandment while in Egypt, choosing to be mistreated rather than being called the son of Pharaoh's daughter. By faith, he identified with God and his people rather than those who were not.

More specifically, Moses 'considered the reproach of Christ greater wealth than the treasures of Egypt, for he was looking to the reward' (Heb. 11:26).

Moses put God first and so looked to the reward that he alone could offer—not the treasures of Egypt but eternal life. Imagine suggesting that God was unhappy with Moses' decision or that it was not good in any sense. Moses was no doubt tempted for immediate, enjoyable glory. But he put God first and suffered as a result. We can never lose when we put God first, even if the immediate consequences may be painful or difficult. This is our hope: that living by faith out of love for God, he will one day reward us for those times we put him first, in situations where even our allegiance to God was tested.

LOVE THE LORD YOUR GOD

All good works must be done in faith, according to the commandments of God. But that is not all. Love for God and Christ must be present if our good works are to be accepted and rewarded.

In one famous example, Mary, the sister of Martha, poured expensive ointment over Christ's head in the presence of others who became indignant. Christ responds to her love by describing her action as a 'beautiful thing' (Mark 14:6). Mary anointed Christ's body for burial in a most extravagant manner. What was her reward? 'And truly, I say to you, wherever the gospel is proclaimed in the whole world, what she has done will be told in memory of her' (Mark 14:9).

WHAT CONSTITUTES GOOD WORKS? | 29

She put Christ before her own personal wealth and comfort. And for that reason, the Savior rewarded her by having her name and deed etched into the Scriptures and church history. Her actions were borne out of faith (pouring expensive ointment) and love (for Christ).

When we obey God out of love, we may receive the same promises the Hebrews received when the author informed them, 'For God is not unjust so as to overlook your work and the love that you have shown for his name in serving the saints, as you still do' (Heb. 6:10). God will not 'overlook' our works done in love towards others for the sake of his name.

Faith, hope, and love are theological virtues that make up the Christian life. It has been said that faith and hope may be exercised with regards to personal advantage, but love always has someone else's benefit in view, whether God or neighbor. God loves to reward love.

DO ALL TO THE GLORY OF GOD

Heidelberg Catechism 91 reads as follows:

Q. What are good works?
A. Only those which are done out of true faith, conform to God's law, and are done for God's glory; and not those based on our own opinion or human tradition.

The Catechism makes an important point: good works must be done for God's glory. As noted above, Christ's glory is one reason why good works are not only desired, but also necessary.

Some reason this way: Doing good works and receiving rewards for our good works may lead to pride. That is true. But we cannot call a work good if we do not live for the glory of God in all that we do. Living for God and Christ remains the best antidote to sinful pride. Pride results when we fail to pursue God's glory in our actions.

The desire to glorify God arises from our love for God, which leads to a good end: the glory of God. There are other ends to good works, such as pursuing our salvation (i.e., entering through the narrow gate that leads to life) and that of others (1 Tim. 4:16). But the highest end is the glory of God.

Christ addresses the problem of 'self' in relation to good works when he castigates the hypocrites for their public displays of their good works: 'Thus, when you give to the needy, sound no trumpet before you, as the hypocrites do in the synagogues and in the streets, that they may be praised by others. Truly, I say to you, they have received their reward' (Matt. 6:2). They wanted their glory and so they 'received their reward,' which was no reward at all.

Some, like the Pharisees, love 'the glory that comes from man more than the glory that comes from God' (John 12:43). They fail to glorify God and so receive glory from men as their reward. We place ourselves in danger when we hypocritically pursue the praise of men but get the frown of God instead. Christ himself had the smile of God, while very often procuring the frown of men. But he knew his reward was with God (Isa. 49:4).

So, whether we pray, drink, laugh, or whatever we do, we must do it for the glory of God. Otherwise, we pursue our own or someone else's glory. Our Savior understood this principle in his own obedience to God the Father: 'I glorified you on earth, having accomplished the work that you gave me to do' (John 17:4).

The reason Christians can do good works is because of who we are in Christ. God has changed the Christian's nature, produced faith in us, and enabled us to express our love for God through obedience.

4

CAN HUMANS MERIT BEFORE GOD?

In light of the clear Scriptural teaching on good works and rewards, one might be tempted to ask, 'Can humans merit a reward from God?' Some recent theologians have tried to defend justification by faith by appealing to the concept of Adamic merit. They believe that Adam's faithful obedience would have merited (earned) the reward of eternal life.

How do we understand the theological concept of merit between humans and God? Could Adam merit anything before God in the Garden? Understanding the first question will help us to answer the second question.

According to the Polish reformed theologian, Johannes Maccovius (1588–1644), for something to be meritorious, four things are required:

1. It must be something that is not owed.
2. It should proceed from the powers of the one who deserves it.
3. The deed/work must somehow benefit the person [i.e., God] who thinks that the act is meritorious.
4. The reward must not be greater than the merit.[6]

The Westminster Assembly divine, Obadiah Sedgwick (1600–1658), similarly suggests that merit:

1. Must be *opus indebitum* ['a non–indebted work']— for he who does do no more than he ought to do, or suffers what he deserves to suffer, merits nothing by his doing, or by his suffering.

2. Must be *opus perfectum* ['a perfect work']—against which no exception can be taken. Nothing is meritorious which is short and faulty.

3. Must be *opus infinitum* ['an infinite work']—a work of infinite value and worth, which cannot only stand before justice, but plead also with it and challenge it for the dignity of what is done or suffered.[7]

These three requirements for a meritorious work are impossible for human beings, especially human beings who have indwelling sin.

Along these lines, in his discussion on the *Westminster Shorter Catechism*, James Fisher maintains that there exists no proportion between Adam's obedience and the life promised. Like so many of his contemporaries and predecessors, he was observing that the life offered by God was of infinitely greater value than the obedience

Adam could have rendered to get it. Adam could not, therefore, merit eternal life. Why? 'Because perfect obedience was no more than what he was bound unto, by virtue of his natural dependence on God.'[8] Anthony Burgess acknowledges that although Adam was in a covenant of works he 'could not merit that happiness which God would bestow upon him.'[9] God's grace to man is 'an infinite good, and all that is done by us is finite.'[10] There will always be a disproportion between our work and God's reward, which therefore rules out meritorious works by us mere humans.

Adam obeyed not in his own strength but in that strength granted by God. Adam was not meant to be the successful Pelagian (obeying purely in his own might!). William Ames, and many other theologians around his time, argued that Adam persisted in the garden by grace and that 'grace was not taken from him before he had sinned.'[11] Ames was not alone in making this point. The acts were truly Adam's, but only because God worked them in him.

In other words, Adam was required to live in obedience towards God, as all mankind must. But his relationship was one of friendship, whereby God enabled ('gifted') him to be a good friend by enabling Adam to possess faith, hope, and love. Adam knew God was good to him in every way. Even if he had received nothing from God, he still could not merit his reward, since Adam's work was still due and it was not infinite. In the end, it is impossible for anyone who depends on God for everything to merit something from him.

CHRIST MERITED GLORY

As the second Adam (Rom 5:14; 1 Cor. 15:45), Christ was, unlike the first Adam, able to merit before God. But Christ was also endowed with the habits of grace in order to keep the terms of the covenant. In other words, in order to keep the Adam–Christ parallels, we must not abandon the concept of grace given to them both, but affirm it. It has been a peculiar oddity that some assume that the parallels between the two Adams mean that Adam could not have received the grace of God because Christ did not. This view is based on the fatal assumption that God was not gracious to Christ in any sense.

There are important Christological reasons why Christ could merit, but Adam could not. If our understanding of what constitutes a meritorious work follows the classical Reformed tradition, the answer is quite simple: the dignity of Christ's person (as the God–man) explains why he, and he alone, could merit before God. He freely performed perfect works, unlike us.

The Father upheld his Son, his servant, by bestowing upon him the Holy Spirit to enable him to perform the work given to him (Isa. 42:1), which flows from the terms of the eternal covenant of redemption.

In Luke's gospel, we read of Christ: 'And the child grew and became strong, filled with wisdom. And the favor (*charis*) of God was upon him...And Jesus increased in wisdom and in stature and in favor (*chariti*) with God and man' (Luke 2:40, 52).

Luke speaks of Jesus increasing in *chariti* (from the

Greek, *charis*). Does this mean 'favor' as many English translations suggest? Or should we translate the Greek as 'grace'? A number of translations render *charis* in Luke 2:40 as grace (e.g., NIV, NASB, KJV). We do not need to get too picky about which word is used, provided we understand that divine grace is not merely God's goodness to the elect in the era of redemptive history. Nor is grace simply offered to those who have sinned. Most of the time, of course, the Scriptures speak of grace in the context of sin, but that is obviously because most of the Scriptures deal with humanity in the context of sin.

God may be 'gracious' to Jesus—not as though he sinned—because God is gracious to his creatures. How much more to his beloved Son? God showed favor to his favorite Son. Christ's human nature was sanctified and filled with graces (Gal. 5:22). As John Owen says, 'For let the natural faculties of the soul, mind, will, and affections, be created pure, innocent, undefiled,—as they cannot be otherwise created immediately by God,—yet there is not enough to enable any rational creature to live to God; much less was it all that was in Jesus Christ.'[12] Likewise, Herman Bavinck notes, 'If humans in general cannot have communion with God except by the Holy Spirit, then this applies even more powerfully to Christ's human nature.'[13]

Merit must be something that is not owed: Christ freely came to obey in our place. Hence, it was not owed. Adam did not freely make the decision to place himself under the law of the covenant of works like Christ did by placing himself under law (Gal. 4:4).

Merit should proceed from the powers of the one who deserves it: Christ relied upon his Father's grace—the grace of the Holy Spirit—but, ontologically speaking, the will and essence of God are one, and therefore Christ's merit proceeded 'from the powers of the one who deserves it.' The Spirit upheld Adam in Eden, but it was not *his* Spirit. Christ was upheld by the Spirit, who is *his* Spirit.

The rewards given to Christ for his meritorious obedience were of use to him because of the glory that would come to his name. God is jealous for his glory, so when Christ merited glory there was no threat of God sharing his glory.

Finally, the rewards given to Christ are proportionate to the work he performed. Adam's reward would have been far greater, assuming we say that Adam would have been granted heavenly life, than what he 'worked for.' Christ's work was under the harshest possible conditions and the work that he did was so great that he received a great reward.

The only way we can speak of Adam 'meriting' is by giving up a classical definition of what constitutes a meritorious work and using the word improperly in terms of what some have called, 'pactum merit' (covenant merit). This phrase is used because Adam clearly could not merit in the strict sense of the term, but he was offered a reward for work accomplished. Whatever terms one decides to use, we must be clear on what we are affirming as well as on what we are denying. Phrases abound in theology, but we must never be content with mere phrases, but always aim to explain what is meant.

Humans can't merit in God's sight because we are creatures and our obedience isn't valuable enough to make God reward us. Because Jesus is God, his obedience is of infinite value and is worthy of reward. Thus, we can't merit, but Jesus can.

WRETCHED MAN THAT I AM!

Since even Adam in his innocence could not merit before God, how much less are we able since we are still sinners? *The Westminster Confession of Faith* makes several important points here in regard to merit (WCF 16.5):

> We cannot by our best works merit pardon of sin, or eternal life at the hand of God, by reason of the great disproportion that is between them and the glory to come; and the infinite distance that is between us and God, whom, by them, we can neither profit, nor satisfy for the debt of our former sins, but when we have done all we can, we have done but our duty, and are unprofitable servants: and because, as they are good, they proceed from His Spirit, and as they are wrought by us, they are defiled, and mixed with so much weakness and imperfection, that they cannot endure the severity of God's judgment.

That is to say, our works are good, but they cannot be meritorious in any sense. Our good works are still defiled and mixed with imperfection and could never, on their own, merit anything from God. Apart from the grace of God, our works, done out of hypocrisy apart from faith, are menstrual cloth (Isa. 64:6).

Incidentally, because we reject human merit, we can affirm that God can and does accept our imperfect works and rewards them. He does not relate to us on the principle of merit, but rather according to grace. He even related to Adam according to grace. True, there was not the grace of mercy, but Adam would only have obeyed perfectly and perpetually because God enabled him to do so. And if Adam had received a reward, it would have been of grace because he could not merit such a reward as eternal life.

5

GOD'S PROMISED REWARDS

Dozens of biblical passages speak of God and Christ rewarding the faithful. This is not a doctrine shrouded in so much mystery that we cannot address it. Christ and the Apostles do not shy away from the idea that God rewards his obedient children. In fact, they speak of rewards freely and frequently, often with the intention of providing motivations for his people to act in this life in order to be rewarded in the one to come.

EACH WILL RECEIVE HIS WAGES

Without getting into the precise nature of the rewards, which is somewhat unknown to us, we can establish the Scriptural teaching that shows God will reward those who obey him. Paul writes to various people, such as husbands, wives, and children. To bondservants, he says, 'Whatever you do, work heartily, as for the Lord and not for men, knowing that from the Lord you will receive the inheritance as your reward. You are serving the Lord Christ' (Col. 3:23–24).

Bondservants who serve Christ faithfully will receive a reward, a recompense for their labor. Bondservants at this time were slaves who obviously had little hope of an earthly inheritance. But Paul promises them something far better—an inheritance from the Lord. The context is clearly not their 'faith alone' as it receives Christ. Rather, the context is that of 'work' whereby there is a gracious 'exchange' (i.e. giving in place of) between the Lord in heaven and his faithful bondservants on earth. In Ephesians, Paul speaks also of promised rewards to others besides bondservants, 'knowing that whatever good anyone does, this he will receive back from the Lord, whether he is a bondservant or is free' (Eph. 6:8).

Perhaps we are not surprised to find God promising rewards to those in difficult circumstances. But what about his attitude towards those who are rich? Do the wealthy content themselves with the fact that their glory will be on earth? Writing to Timothy, Paul exhorts the rich to 'do good, to be rich in good works' (1 Tim. 6:18). Why? Because, by setting their hope on God instead of the uncertainty of riches, they store up treasure for themselves (1 Tim. 6:19). God will reward even the rich if they will serve God, not money, first.

Again, as in the case of the bondservants, a reward

is promised in the context of obedience. Paul aims to motivate the rich to act wisely with their wealth. He holds out to them true 'financial planning' in the sense that their work for the kingdom now will result in treasure in the heaven to come.

In the Gospel accounts, Christ speaks frequently about rewards. For example, in Matthew 10, he speaks of rewards for specific actions (Matt. 10:40–42):

> Whoever receives you receives me, and whoever receives me receives him who sent me. The one who receives a prophet because he is a prophet will receive a prophet's reward, and the one who receives a righteous person because he is a righteous person will receive a righteous person's reward. And whoever gives one of these little ones even a cup of cold water because he is a disciple, truly, I say to you, he will by no means lose his reward.

We should be thankful to God for these words uttered by his Son. Not all of us can be 'prophets.' But we can play a role in God's purposes and share in the rewards offered to his special servants. His people can 'help' his faithful prophets and so share in the reward offered to them. The same remains true for receiving a 'righteous person' by giving what appears to be a small gift (cup of cold water) to an insignificant person ('little ones'). God rewards even 'small' deeds, not just 'great' ones.

The concept of God rewarding the righteous is found in many places throughout the Old Testament. After Saul recognized his sin against David by trying to kill him, David responded (1 Sam. 26:22–24):

> And David answered and said, 'Here is the spear, O king! Let one of the young men come over and take it. The LORD rewards every man for his righteousness and his faithfulness, for the LORD gave you into my hand today, and I would not put out my hand against the LORD's anointed. Behold, as your life was precious this day in my sight, so may my life be precious in the sight of the LORD, and may he deliver me out of all tribulation.

David speaks of the LORD rewarding every man for his righteousness and faithfulness. David clearly expected to be rewarded by God for this, as he does in Psalm 18. We might pause here and ask whether we are a little embarrassed by his words. Are these appropriate for New Covenant Christians (Ps. 18:20–24)?

> The LORD dealt with me according to my righteousness;
>> according to the cleanness of my hands he rewarded me.
> For I have kept the ways of the LORD,
>> and have not wickedly departed from my God.
> For all his rules were before me,
>> and his statutes I did not put away from me.
> I was blameless before him,
>> and I kept myself from my guilt.
> So the LORD has rewarded me according to my righteousness,
>> according to the cleanness of my hands in his sight.

The context here concerns sanctification, not justification. David speaks of the LORD rewarding him for his righteousness. Of course, David, perhaps more than anyone in the Old Testament, understood his sinfulness

(Ps. 32). To the same degree, he also understood God's grace (Ps. 51). Hence, he can speak in this manner not simply because he is righteous, but because God is gracious in his estimation of David's imperfections.

Humans can't merit in God's sight because we are creatures and our obedience isn't valuable enough to make God reward us. Because Jesus is God, his obedience is of infinite value and is worthy of reward. Thus, we can't merit, but Jesus can.

6

REWARDS AND PRAYER

Prayer is one of the most difficult tasks of the Christian life. This struggle doesn't just exist for immature Christians or those very weak in faith. The testimonies of even some great Christians verify that prayer is difficult.

'Everything we do in the Christian life is easier than prayer.' (Martyn Lloyd–Jones)[14]

'There is nothing that we are so bad at all our days as prayer.' (Alexander Whyte)[15]

Given the difficulty of prayer, how does Christ motivate us to it? In Matthew 6:6, he promises his disciples their Father will reward them for what they do (i.e. pray) in secret. Notice how often the word 'reward' appears in that chapter alone.

We do have to ask whether we adequately believe such

words. Do we really believe, as we should, that God will reward us? If we did, we would spend a lot more time in secret prayer. We do not have because we do not ask! We do not ask because we lack faith (Matt. 21:22).

Faith exists as the hand that begs from God: 'And without faith it is impossible to please him, for whoever would draw near to God must believe that he exists and that he rewards those who seek him' (Heb. 11:6). Christ, the man of faith par excellence, certainly grasped this concept in his own prayer life. In fact, he prayed for his reward: 'And now, Father, glorify me in your own presence with the glory that I had with you before the world existed' (John 17:5).

I don't know precisely how the Lord will reward us for what we do in secret. Sometimes the answers to prayer are obvious or immediate. Sometimes he rewards us by not giving us what we (sometimes wrongly) ask for. And there are prayers that may not even be answered in our own lifetime. For example, Stephen's prayer in Acts 7:59–60 may have resulted in the conversion of Saul of Tarsus. Or perhaps Moses' prayer to see God's glory in Exodus 33:18 was answered at the Transfiguration, long after Moses had gone to glory.

We do know, however, that the rewards for our prayers are of grace. As Matthew Henry says, 'It is called a reward, but it is of grace, not of debt; what merit can there be in begging?'[16] God has promised to reward his children when they pray in secret, and that motivation alone should be enough to get us into our 'prayer closets' where we ask in order to receive. It is true, that if I could change God's mind through my prayers then I would not pray. But we can still accomplish God's purposes through prayer because he ordained matters that way. Our reward is knowing, first, that we possess the privilege to ask God for anything. We may receive our reward in this lifetime or in the life to come.

Why should God reward our prayers? Because all true prayer is in the Spirit (Rom. 8:26–27):

> Likewise the Spirit helps us in our weakness. For we do not know what to pray for as we ought, but the Spirit himself intercedes for us with groanings too deep for words. And he who searches hearts knows what is the mind of the Spirit, because the Spirit intercedes for the saints according to the will of God.

When we pray in the Spirit, we will pray according to God's will, which pleases him. So if the Spirit helps us, God will be especially pleased because our work is his work. In a sense, God rewards his own works in us.

Prayer is a difficult practice for Christians. However, God is pleased when we pray and rewards us. How does this truth encourage you to spend more time with your heavenly Father in prayer?

7

JUDGMENT ACCORDING TO WORKS

The idea that Christ will judge Christians does not sit well with many in the church today. Many regard such a judgment with terror, especially given our knowledge of our sins—some of which are particularly heinous.

We cannot deny, however, that Christians will be judged according to works when Christ returns. Sometimes we need to be confronted with the word of God and its plain teaching by pausing to read what God has to say about the judgment to come. Here are a few passages that teach a future judgment according to works:

I the LORD search the heart and test the mind, to give every man according to his ways, according to the fruit of his deeds (Jer. 17:10).

For we must all appear before the judgment seat of Christ, so that each one may receive what is due for what he has done in the body, whether good or evil (2 Cor. 5:10).

For the Son of Man is going to come with his angels in the glory of his Father, and then he will repay each person according to what he has done (Matt. 16:27).

…for an hour is coming when all who are in the tombs will hear his voice and come out, those who have done good to the resurrection of life, and those who have done evil to the resurrection of judgment (John 5:28–29).

And the sea gave up the dead who were in it, Death and Hades gave up the dead who were in them, and they were judged, each one of them, according to what they had done (Rev. 20:13).

Behold, I am coming soon, bringing my recompense with me, to repay each one for what he has done (Rev. 22:12).

The question arises, how do we reconcile such teaching with the doctrine of justification by faith alone? We obviously do not embrace the Roman Catholic version of 'two justifications.' We hold to one justification by faith, but we must also grapple with the nature of true, saving faith, and the not too infrequent conditional language of the New Testament (see WCF 13.1, citing Heb. 12:14; 2 Cor. 7:1). In relation to faith, John Owen says:

For there is a faith whereby we are justified, which he who has shall be assuredly saved, which purifies the heart and works by love. And there is a faith or believing, which does nothing of all this; which [he] who has, and has no more, is not justified, nor can be saved.[17]

This concept forms the backbone of the judgment according to works (see also WCF 11.2).

Justification has an 'authoritative' and a 'declarative' (or 'demonstrative') aspect. Thomas Goodwin points out that 'the one [i.e. authoritative] is the justification of men's persons *coram Deo*, before God, as they appear before him nakedly, and have to do with him alone for the right to salvation; and so they are justified by faith without works' (Rom. 4:2–5).[18]

But there is a demonstrative aspect to our justification. According to Goodwin, God will, at the Day of Judgment, judge men and 'put a difference between man and man, and that upon this account, that the one were true believers when he justified them; the other were unsound, even in their very acts of faith.' Simon the Magician 'believed' but his act of faith was spurious—that of the hypocrite (Acts 8:13, 'Even Simon himself believed'). God will therefore make evident, for all to see, the difference between those truly justified and those under wrath, even though they may have 'professed' faith.

Matthew 25:31–46 is instructive on this point. Christ will return and make a separation of the wicked and the righteous. The language of the passage makes clear that the distinction is based upon the actions of the wicked and the righteous. But the chapter also has in view the visible church:

'For I was hungry and you gave me food, I was thirsty and you gave me drink, I was a stranger and you welcomed me, I was naked and you clothed me, I was sick and you visited me,

I was in prison and you came to me.' Then the righteous will answer him, saying, 'Lord, when did we see you hungry and feed you, or thirsty and give you drink? And when did we see you a stranger and welcome you, or naked and clothe you? And when did we see you sick or in prison and visit you?' And the King will answer them, 'Truly, I say to you, as you did it to one of the least of these my brothers, you did it to me.'

The wicked, those on Christ's left, are chastised for not doing good works. The wicked forgot that not doing good works to the most insignificant in Christ's name is the same as if they had not given him food or water in his time of need (see Matt. 10:40-42; 25:41–46).

The parable of the net (i.e., kingdom of heaven) in Matthew 13 proves that the church is mixed with the true versus the false (Matt. 13:47–50):

Again, the kingdom of heaven is like a net that was thrown into the sea and gathered fish of every kind. When it was full, men drew it ashore and sat down and sorted the good into containers but threw away the bad. So it will be at the end of the age. The angels will come out and separate the evil from the righteous and throw them into the fiery furnace. In that place there will be weeping and gnashing of teeth.

Good works are not optional for the Christian. True faith works through love (Gal. 5:6).

The way we understand the relationship of good works to salvation is through the Reformed distinction between the 'right' versus 'possession'. Herman Witsius gives a brief but accurate explanation of this distinction: the 'practice of Christian piety is the way to life, because thereby we go to the possession of the right obtained by Christ.'[19] The right to life is 'assigned to the obedience of Christ, that all the value of our holiness may be entirely excluded.' Regarding the possession of life, however, 'our works…which the Spirit of Christ works in us, and by us, contribute something to the latter.'[20]

Thomas Goodwin, who affirmed salvation by faith alone, also posits: God will not 'put the *possession* of salvation upon that private act of his own, without having anything else to show for it.'[21] Christians possess the right to heaven because of the work of Christ, yet the means by which they obtain heaven are by the good works performed in this life, as prepared by God (Eph. 2:10). In a manner very similar to Goodwin, Petrus van Mastricht notes, 'God does not want to grant the possession of eternal life, unless there are, next to faith, also good works which precede this *possession*, Heb. 12:14; Matt. 7:21; 25:34–36; Rom. 2:7, 10.'[22] To this list of eminent theologians could be added many more.

At the final judgment, God will justify himself. He justifies sinners apart from works, but he will also demonstrate the difference between the faithful and the wicked. It will be a public display as he justifies his own acts of justification. Or, to put the matter another way, God will justify the faith of the justified believer. The judgment will prove those with a lively faith that worked through love. Remember, good works will accompany faith (WCF 11.2).

Being judged by works at the final day differs not from being justified by works at that time, so long as we understand that the justification of our works at the final day is a public demonstration of our faith working through love. Christ speaks of a (demonstrative) justification according to works: 'I tell you, on the day of judgment people will give account for every careless word they speak, for by your words you will be justified, and by your words you will be condemned' (Matt. 12:36–37). The word 'justified' is used by our Lord himself in the context of works. Without giving way to Roman Catholicism, we must understand this as a demonstrative justification. Paul does not teach a 'faith alone' position, but a justification 'by faith alone.' Many Roman Catholics (and indeed some Protestants) wrongly critique the Reformation doctrine because they think we hold to a 'faith alone' view, which is actually antinomian. We become Christians by faith alone, but our faith is never alone in the Christian life.

God will judge us in a manner proclaimed by others as righteous. Theoretically, the whole world should be able to view a true believer's justification and verify true faith 'not alone in the person justified,' but 'ever accompanied with all other saving graces,' as 'no dead faith,' but one that 'works by love' (WCF 11.2, citing James 2:17; Gal. 5:6). The final judgment concerns the vindication of the triune God just as much as that of the lives of true believers.

A Christian's standing before God is not based on their works. But a Christian performs such to demonstrate standing in Christ. Obedience doesn't make one but indeed proves one as a Christian.

NO CONDEMNATION NOW

Should the doctrine of a judgment according to works cause people to despair? No, since there is 'therefore no condemnation for those who are in Christ Jesus' (Rom. 8:1). Nonetheless, hypocrites should be afraid. Christ condemns hypocrites in the church (Matt. 25:41–46) as those exposed for their absence of good works and who neglect the weightier matters of the law (Matt. 23:23). Those in the Spirit will have the grace of assurance, whereas those in the flesh cannot possess it.

Here is the good news for those who have a true, lively faith: the resurrection will precede the judgment (*Larger Catechism* 88; 2 Cor. 5:10). Based on 1 John 3:2, we shall see Christ and be immediately transformed by the sight of him. We shall appear then, in a manner of speaking, as already justified at the judgment. Remember, when we first believed, we received the 'right to life.' This is the glory of justification (Rom. 5:1; 8:1). Nothing can separate us from God's love, especially at the judgment.

We do not need to fear the final judgment if we are children of God. But as children of God, glorified in the presence of Christ, we 'must [nevertheless] all appear before the judgment seat of Christ, so that each one may receive what is due for what he has done in the body, whether good or evil' (2 Cor. 5:10). Indeed, some in the church will fail at the final judgment, because their faith was dead (i.e., did not produce fruit, John 15:2–5, 10, 16).

I believe that some speak of the final judgment in a sub–trinitarian way, as they focus only on declarative justification. That certainly gives the right to life. Only the imputed righteousness of Christ can withstand the severity of God's judgment. But, demonstrative justification, as I have highlighted above, is the Father's approval of the Spirit's work—that is, the Spirit of Christ (Rom. 8:9)—in his people because of our union with the Savior. God is not so much looking down upon us and saying we are good enough, but rather vindicating the work of his Son, who sends the Spirit into our hearts to make us like Christ (Rom. 8:29).

The Father who gave two gifts to us, the Son and the Spirit, will look upon us as justified in Christ and sanctified in him by the Spirit. Our Heavenly Father will be well pleased with his work. He will accept us for Christ's sake and reward and vindicate us because of his Spirit, who enabled us to do good works and prepared us for them in advance (Eph. 2:10).

In my opinion, we need to do a better job—at least, from what I've been able to read—of describing the final judgment in explicitly trinitarian terms. To that end, the account above aims to do that.

If there exists a more coherent way to bridge together the freeness of justification by faith, the conditional language of Scripture (Rom. 8:13), and the fact that Christians will be judged according to deeds done in the body (2 Cor. 5:10), I would welcome it. But we need to be able to deal with all that the Scriptures teach, otherwise we open ourselves up to accusations of failing to take them seriously.

8

REWARDING OUR CHILDREN ON EARTH

God helps us to understand the concept of a father rewarding his children through our own parenting. Thus, we can draw some general principles for parenting from the way God the Father treats his children. That is why I am not, in principle, opposed to various types of punishments for our children when they are disobedient. A spanking may be the best, most appropriate way to deal with sin in our young children (Prov. 23:13), but withholding privileges, for example, may also be a suitable punishment. God did that with his people in the Old Testament (Ps. 95:11).

What about promising our children rewards for obedience, with the intention of motivating them to do what we ask? Here, I believe, we may look at the way in which God rewards his children and appropriately, with great care and wisdom, apply this principle to the way we raise our own children.

Given the plethora of teaching in Scripture on rewards for good works (Rev. 22:12; Matt. 16:27; 25:14–30; Luke 19:11–27; 2 Cor. 5:10; Heb. 11:26), I am surprised the topic does not surface more often. The issue is not whether God rewards our good works, but can rewards for good works motivate us in any way?

It may be that some think that promising rewards for obedience leads to a slavish spirit. Anticipating this objection, John Owen acknowledges that some think 'to yield holy obedience unto God with respect unto rewards and punishments is servile, and becomes not the free spirit of the children of God.'[23]

In response to this objection, Owen asserts that such a reaction is a 'vain' imagination. Only the bondage of our spirits can make what we do servile. 'But,' says Owen, 'a due respect unto God's promises and threatenings is a principal part of our liberty.'[24] He argues that in the new covenant the hope of rewards, for example, is actually a liberating motive for holiness.

Those who are partakers of the covenant of grace, and make use of the means of grace that God has appointed for believers, may find comfort in the fact that they will not fail to perform the obedience required by God 'merely for want of power and spiritual strength' (see 2 Pet. 1:3; Matt. 11:30; 1 John 5:3).[25]

The fact that God promises rewards to his children will necessarily motivate them to seek these rewards. How could we be indifferent to such promises? We would be disobedient children if we did not, in some measure, seek that which is so clearly promised in God's word.

How, then, does this relate to parenting? Parents, if they are able, naturally want to bless and reward their children. There is always a fine line between good theology and bad theology, and that line is perhaps a lot finer than we'd like to imagine. Some parents get their children to obey only by either promising or threatening something. The latter may be effective only when issued with a harsh tone and loud voice. Sometimes motivating children amounts to nothing more than perpetual bribery, which ends up enslaving not only the parents, but also the children.

Our children need to be motivated to obey simply because they know that such pleases the Lord (Col. 3:20). Thus, we endanger our children and ourselves if we get them to do something just because something else is promised. Yet, that does not prohibit motivating our children by sometimes promising them a reward for their obedience. Godly wisdom from the parents will, of course, dictate the frequency and nature of the reward, but the principle itself is a way—not the way—to help our children obey.

Returning to my original point, our Heavenly Father promises rewards for things done during this life, assuming they truly constitute good works. While we need to be careful in this matter, I think parents should do the same for their children. They must learn to reward their children in appropriate ways, to tangibly teach them how our

Heavenly Father acts towards his children. There exist not only many unconditional but also conditional ('if you do this then…') promises and warnings for God's people.

Expecting our children to obey without ever promising a reward may provoke them to wrath. In this way, earthly parents fail to model their Heavenly Father. God loves his children and delights to reward them for their imperfect obedience. Should we be any different with our own children?

 God rewards his children's works, as imperfect as they are. How should this affect the way you treat your children?

9

LAYING UP PEOPLE IN HEAVEN

As we read the various commands Christ taught his disciples during his earthly ministry, we ought to meditate on how he kept them himself. Such reflection can open up Scripture in fresh and exciting ways. For example, in the Sermon on the Mount, Christ gives the following command (Matt. 6:19–21):

> Do not lay up for yourselves treasures on earth, where moth and rust destroy and where thieves break in and steal, but lay up for yourselves treasures in heaven, where neither moth nor rust destroys and where thieves do not break in and steal. For where your treasure is, there your heart will be also.

Christians must lay up for themselves treasures in heaven. Did Christ, the pioneer of our faith (Heb. 12:2), keep this command? And if so, how? He principally kept this command by laying *us* up for himself in heaven (John 10:10). We are his treasured possession (Deut. 7:6). He raised us up, where we are seated with him (Col. 3:1; Eph. 2:6). In this way, as in all things, he and the Father have the same purpose and will, namely, to lay up people (i.e. treasures) for themselves in heaven: '[God's] glorious inheritance in the saints' (Eph. 1:18).

There are a number of ways in which we can keep this command. While Christ procured salvation, the application of salvation to sinners usually involves human agents (Rom. 10:14). So there is a sense in which we too lay up for ourselves treasures in heaven by sharing the Word of life with an unbelieving world (Phil. 2:16).

Wives can lay up for themselves treasures in heaven according to Peter's command in 1 Peter 3:1–2, 'Likewise, wives, be subject to your own husbands, so that even if some do not obey the word, they may be won without a word by the conduct of their wives, when they see your respectful and pure conduct.'

Pastors can lay up for themselves treasures in heaven according to Paul's command to Timothy in 1 Timothy 4:16, 'Keep a close watch on yourself and on the teaching. Persist in this, for by so doing you will save both yourself and your hearers.'

Believers can live such godly lives that unbelievers will be won to the kingdom: 'Keep your conduct among the Gentiles honorable, so that when they speak against you as evildoers, they may see your good deeds and glorify God on the day of visitation' (1 Pet. 2:12). The day of 'visitation' likely concerns the day of conversion, not the final day when Christ returns. Elsewhere, Christ says, '...let your light shine before others, so that they may see your good works and give glory to your Father who is in heaven' (Matt. 5:16).

Parents can play a role in bringing salvation to their children: 'Fathers, do not provoke your children to anger, but bring them up in the discipline and instruction of the Lord' (Eph. 6:4). Parents commit the error of hyper–Calvinism by thinking our actions (or lack thereof) have no effect on our children's salvation. While salvation clearly comes by the Lord's grace alone, he uses means to accomplish it. We will reap what we sow, if we leave our children home from church, fail to read and discuss the Bible with them, pray with and for them, or neglect to lovingly discipline them. But, in dependence upon God's grace, if we do what we should in these areas, we may be confident that God will use these ordained means to bring about their salvation. Sadly, even the best parents sometimes have to deal with prodigals. Still, God promises blessings to faithful parents who must never think their diligence matters not.

When we return to Matthew 6:19–21, we can understand this passage in a way that keeps us from becoming self-centered about our rewards/treasures in heaven. Our treasures in heaven will include God's people, just

God uses a Christian's life as a testimony of his power and work in the lives of others. Think about practical ways this should change how you interact with unbelievers.

as Christ's does. But, remarkably, we even have a role to play in 'laying up people/treasures in heaven.'

I have heard many appeals for why we should evangelize. 'People are going to Hell.' True enough. 'God is not worshipped.' Indeed. But we may also say that we have an obligation, as Christ did, to lay up for ourselves treasures (i.e. souls) in heaven, which is a great part of our reward. Heaven will be a family of people who are in every way a treasured possession, not only to Christ, but also to us. Do we, in our evangelism, tell people we want to spend eternity with them in heaven?

Christ's whole life involved missionary activity. Adam was God's treasured possession, and though he sinned, he remained such a treasure. How would God himself lay up Adam in heaven? Through Christ, who in turn enjoys Adam in heaven because the Father desires to enjoy him there as well. Adam, like each redeemed saint, manifests the bond of love between the Father and the Son.

We are also told that where our treasure is our heart will be also (Matt. 6:21). Where is the heart of Christ in heaven? It is towards sinners on earth and the redeemed in heaven because we are his treasure—those whom he personally carries to the Father. So I'd like to think that when Christ issued this command to his disciples, he knew that he would be laying them up for himself in heaven. Why? Because, his heart was with them.

What a joyous reward: to have eternal friendships begun on earth through various God-appointed means for the salvation of his people. Our union with each other can be very close on earth, but how much more in heaven and the new heavens and earth. There we will be absent of sin and filled with the Spirit. I look forward to perfectly satisfying and rewarding friendships in heaven begun on earth through the spread of the gospel from one person to another.

10

DIFFERING GLORIES IN HEAVEN

Though all Christians are justified by the same righteousness, not all are equally sanctified. Progressive
sanctification entails degrees of holiness in an individual
as he or she dies to sin and lives to righteousness, which
occurs in varying levels and rates among God's people.
For example, not all perform the exact same amount
of good works with the same consistency, sincerity, or
purity. Such variation is manifested also in the fact that
God's people live for different lengths of time. Consider
the thief on the cross who, upon his conversion, entered
glory with less than a day for sanctifying grace to
transform his life. With varying degrees of sanctification
in mind, should we expect degrees of glory in heaven?
The Scriptures seem to affirm this.

In his extended discourse on the resurrection body in 1 Corinthians 15, Paul makes the following statement in connection with the resurrection body: 'There is one glory of the sun, and another glory of the moon, and another glory of the stars; for star differs from star in glory. So is it with the resurrection of the dead…' (1 Cor. 15:41–42).

Now, without question, Christ 'will transform our lowly body to be like his glorious body' (Phil. 3:21). But that does not mean we will possess the exact glory of Christ, for he is the God-man. His body is in union with his divine nature. So Paul does not suggest an exact like-for-like body. Hence, we will all have glorious bodies like Christ's, without sharing the exact glory of the glorious One. With that in mind, even among God's resurrected saints, we can expect degrees of glory according to Paul's language in 1 Corinthians 15:41–42.

As the heavenly bodies differ in glory, so the bodies of resurrected saints will differ in glory. All Christians rightly enter heaven based upon the mediatorial work of Christ. This does not imply sharing the same glory there. Our works will follow us and we will all possess a unique glory based upon our good works done in the flesh.

THOSE WHO TURN MANY TO RIGHTEOUSNESS

The pastoral ministry remains difficult for faithful shepherds seeking to love the sheep. Opportunists who

Francis Turretin states, 'To religious teachers is promised a peculiar glory above those to be saved by their instrumentality.'[26]

take advantage of and fleece the sheep seem to do so with the greatest ease. They will suffer loss and may even face judgment.

Paul speaks in 1 Corinthians about works and rewards: 'If the work that anyone has built on the foundation survives, he will receive a reward. If anyone's work is burned up, he will suffer loss, though he himself will be saved, but only as through fire' (1 Cor. 3:14–15).

The immediate context does not explicitly tell us what determines whether a person's work will be rewarded and thus escape judgment. The context and the rest of God's Word, however, proves helpful (1 Tim. 4:16).

Those who build on the foundation laid by Paul (1 Cor. 3:10–11) will have their work judged. Paul's own work will meet the required criteria since his work is foundational. His earlier comments to the Corinthians bear this out as he preached in weakness, demonstrating the power of the gospel and Christ in him. Likewise, he spoke not with human wisdom, but with God's (1 Cor. 2:6–7). Hence, the foundation he lays is the gospel. Human innovations, in the context of the church and gospel ministry, will be burnt. But faithfulness to God's word in the gospel ministry will be rewarded.

Paul later parallels what he has said earlier in 3:10–11 as he considers his own life and ministry (1 Cor. 4:4–5):

For I am not aware of anything against myself, but I am not thereby acquitted. It is the Lord who judges me. Therefore do not pronounce judgment before the time, before the Lord comes, who will bring to light the things now hidden in darkness and will disclose the purposes of the heart. Then each one will receive his commendation from God.

Paul acknowledges that God will judge him. Interestingly, he manifests no casual attitude about this judgment as if it were no big deal. In fact, he says that God will 'disclose the purposes of the heart' (v. 5). Many Christian leaders, pastors, and theologians outwardly say and accomplish seemingly great things, but God will examine their heart motive. 'Some indeed preach Christ from envy and rivalry, but others from good will' (Phil. 1:15).

God will not only judge the wicked, but also Christians, and among them ministers of the gospel. Unfaithfulness to God forfeits rewards from him: 'He who plants and he who waters are one, and each will receive his wages according to his labor...If the work that anyone has built on the foundation survives, he will receive a reward' (1 Cor. 3:8, 14).

We might be tempted to say the reward simply denotes salvation. But that position undermines justification by faith alone. Faith alone gives us the right to salvation. We receive eternal life when we believe. Therefore, it is much more preferable, for the sake of the gospel, and in the interests of the Reformation principles we adhere to as Protestants, to argue that Paul here treats rewards above and beyond eternal life. His language in 1 Corinthians 3:15 makes this clear: the minister's work will 'suffer loss' but 'he himself will be saved, but only as through fire.' In other words, the worker for God, while gaining heaven, will truly lose something in the process.

Beyond this, we might say he makes such an entrance 'by the skin of his teeth.'

Even this view magnifies God's grace. Someone can be unfaithful in their work, to a certain degree, but still enter heaven. Only they will lose the rewards promised to workers who build on the foundation laid by the Apostles and Prophets (Eph. 2:20). Someone might say, 'If I just make it to heaven that's all that matters, so pardon me if I am not as zealous and dedicated as I could be.' Such a response fails to understand the responsibility we have as the children of God to faithfully serve the one who so graciously saves us.

A Christian's standing before God is not based on their works, but a Christian performs good works to demonstrate their standing in Christ. Obedience doesn't make one a Christian, but proves one to be a Christian.

BECAUSE YOU HAVE BEEN FAITHFUL

The Parable of the Talents in Matthew 25 possesses eschatological force. In other words, Christ offers a parable with heavenly consequences. Like all parables, its meaning is not immediately obvious. I am persuaded that Matthew 25 expands upon Paul's thoughts in 1 Corinthians 3–4.

The Master in the parable is Christ, the Son of Man. The servants are his disciples who have been given specific 'talents.' The talents are, specifically, a reference to the knowledge of kingdom mysteries given especially to his disciples (see Matt. 13:11–13). Those with such understanding are to be faithful stewards of those mysteries (see 1 Cor. 4:1) and will be rewarded for it. Unfaithfulness will result in judgment.

In the parable of the talents in Matthew, the Master (Christ) rewards the faithful by saying: 'I will set you over much.' In Luke's Gospel, the parable of the Ten Minas gives a further indication regarding diversity of reward for faithfulness (Luke 19:17–19):

> And he said to him, 'Well done, good servant! Because you have been faithful in a very little, you shall have authority over ten cities.' And the second came, saying, 'Lord, your mina has made five minas.' And he said to him, 'And you are to be over five cities.'

Turretin observes from this parable, 'He who gained five [minas] is placed over ten cities and he who gained two, over two. This could not be said unless there was granted a diversity of reward corresponding in a certain proportion to the disparity of labor.'[27]

The original hearers were promised rewards for faithful stewardship of kingdom mysteries, once concealed only to be revealed. Matthew's readers of all ages are faced with a similar exhortation and promise of reward.

In heaven, then, some will have greater 'rule' and responsibility. They will therefore have a greater glory, because they were faithful on earth with the 'talents' God gave them. The parables of the talents and minas teach us that no one is without talents. Yet, to whom much is given, much is expected (Luke 12:48).

Christ received the most talents, and he was the most

faithful. Thus, his reward will reflect his talents and faithfulness. Because of our union with Christ, we share in this reality. God graciously rewards faithfulness to his name and honor. By faith, we believe that what we do now has real consequences for our heavenly existence. Of course, and this cannot be stressed enough, we cannot merit or earn salvation. But that does not mean we should, out of fear for compromising justification by faith alone, jettison all talk of rewards for faithfulness. The Scriptures speak frequently and sometimes with great perspicuity about rewards. Are we wiser than God by failing to speak and preach on these matters?

God gives gifts to all of his children for them to use in service of him and his church. As we are responsible for our stewardship of God's gifts, think about ways you can utilize such for his service.

11

REWARDS IN THIS LIFE

When we discuss the doctrine of rewards, we must take care not to limit such to our heavenly existence, particularly in the new heavens and the new earth. Our lives are cross-shaped, which means Christians will never be strangers to suffering. But that does not mean that all we do is suffer. God rewards us here on earth as a foretaste of his plan to bless us for all eternity.

One reward we receive as a result of our obedience is an increased presence of God's love of complacency. We must be very careful in stating the matter this way, since this is a doctrine with a rich historical pedigree, but barely treated today for a number of reasons.

We can speak of God's voluntary (free) love towards his people. This has three components:

1. God's love of benevolence, whereby he elects us in Christ and predestines us to eternal life;
2. God's love of beneficence, whereby he wills all things in time to bring about the salvation of the elect;
3. God's love of delight (friendship), also understood historically as his love of complacency, whereby he rewards people according to their holiness.

One of the best theologians from the seventeenth century, Melchior Leydekker (1624–1721), of the Netherlands, distinguishes between God's benevolent love and his complacent love in the following manner:

> God's love is either of benevolence or of complacency. The first is the love by which God shall do well to the elect, before there is anything in them that could give Him complacency, John 3:16, Rom. 5:8. And therefore, it can be regarded either as predetermining in God's decrees, or as actually effecting in time. The second, the love of complacency, is the case where God approves the good which is in the elect, especially as being commanded by him and caused, Heb. 11:5–6; John 14:21; 16:26–27.[28]

As Leydekker makes clear, God's benevolent love is logically prior to his complacent love. It has to be this way, since God's love of benevolence is the fountain of election and all blessings the elect receive. The love of complacency delights in the good present in his elect, which exists only because of his benevolent love. The Puritan theologian, Stephen Charnock, also makes reference to this distinction in God's love:

If God loves holiness in a lower measure, much more will he love it in a higher degree, because then his image is more illustrious and beautiful, and comes nearer to the lively lineaments of his own infinite purity...(John 14:21)... He loves a holy man for some resemblance to him in his nature; but when there is an abounding in sanctified dispositions suitable to it, there is an increase of favor; the more we resemble the original, the more shall we enjoy the blessedness of that original: as any partake more of the Divine likeness, they partake more of the Divine happiness.[29]

Interestingly, both Leydekker and Charnock appeal to the same passage, John 14:21, which reads: 'Whoever has my commandments and keeps them, he it is who loves me. And he who loves me will be loved by my Father, and I will love him and manifest myself to him.' This passage cannot refer to God's unconditional love because that would mean his love only comes to us if we keep his commandments, which would make our law-keeping a qualification for receiving his electing love. Instead, this is speaking about his love of friendship (complacency), whereby Christ manifests more of his covenantal presence to those who keep his commandments.

In discussing the doctrine of justification, Turretin notes the language of John 14:23, where Christ promises the love of the Father to those who love Christ, 'not affectively and as to its beginning (as if the love of the Father then begins, since he loved us before, 1 John 4:10), but effectively and as to continuance *and increase* because he will prove his love by distinguished blessings and console them by a new manifestation of himself.'[30]

Keeping Christ's commandments brings a great reward: the increased manifestation of his presence in our lives. We can have confidence that his love of benevolence is unconditional and we shall always be children of God, but why should we not also strive to enjoy more of the manifestation of his love in our lives?

SOW BOUNTIFULLY, REAP BOUNTIFULLY

Paul's wondrously pastoral section on giving in 2 Corinthians 8–9 reveals that the good work of giving to the church cannot go unrewarded. In 2 Corinthians 9:6, he explains to his readers, 'whoever sows sparingly will also reap sparingly, and whoever sows bountifully will also reap bountifully.' This clearly affirms the basic argument of this book, namely, 'whatever one sows, that will he also reap' (Gal. 6:7, 9). Paul applies the general principle to Christian giving: 'Each one must give as he has decided in his heart' (2 Cor. 9:7). Those who give freely from the heart receive this reward: 'God loves a cheerful giver' (2 Cor. 9:7). I take this 'love' to be the love of complacency, described above. As Spurgeon argues in his sermon on this text, 'Remember, this is not a sentence spoken to all sorts of men; this was addressed to the members of a Christian church. God loves them all, but He has special *complacency* in those whom, by His grace, He has taught to be cheerful givers.'[31]

But the reward does not end with the reception of God's fatherly favor. In fact, Paul says in verses 10–11, 'He who supplies seed to the sower and bread for food will supply and multiply your seed for sowing and increase the harvest of your righteousness. You will be enriched in every way to be generous in every way, which through us will produce thanksgiving to God.'

A number of promises offered in verses 10–11 result from freely giving money to kingdom work. First, many properly critical of the 'health, wealth, and prosperity' gospel (which is no gospel at all), probably experience discomfort with verse 10. Here, Paul seems to be saying that if we give (money), God increases our seed (money) for sowing. When we give, God does not promise to make us rich but to enable us to give more. That is a reward in this life that has kingdom values guiding our actions and works. Second, giving will 'increase the harvest of [our] righteousness,' which means that God rewards giving from a pure heart and good motive. He rewards us by increasing our righteousness. Giving out of faith to the Lord's work allows growth in grace. By being generous, we become even more generous. Third, our generosity should ordinarily cause others to rejoice with thanksgiving to God. In other words, our good works lead other Christians to praise God.

So much of Paul's encouragement to give to the work of the kingdom focuses on rewards reaped in this lifetime. God is no miser who demands, 'Wait for it all in heaven.' He gives rewards and blessings now because, as a Father, he cannot help but reward his children for their sincere obedience.

AN EXCELLENT WIFE

Keeping the commandments always benefits us more than breaking them. For example, the seventh commandment, tells us to 'not commit' adultery (Exod. 20:14). We see the positive side of this commandment in Ephesians 5:25, 'Now as the church submits to Christ, so also wives should submit in everything to their husbands. Husbands, love your wives, as Christ loved the church and gave himself up for her.'

A husband loving his wife loves himself (Eph. 5:28), as a reward. To obey and receive in the act of obeying means that faithfulness to God's law necessarily rewards the righteous. While there are exceptions, a husband loving his wife will ordinarily enjoy a happier, fulfilled, stable, loving marriage. As people glibly quip, 'a happy wife is a happy life'—a saying with much truth, indeed. A husband who refuses to love his wife sacrificially asks for trouble.

Likewise, a godly and submissive wife (Eph. 5:24), who respects her husband, will ordinarily be rewarded with a loving husband in return. In my view, the primary responsibility comes upon the husband to love his wife, but the wife also has responsibilities to him. Those play a role in helping him to be a more loving husband. So, obeying the seventh commandment, for example, brings with it obvious temporal blessings and rewards. I do not mean to be crass, but a loving husband will generally find his wife more willing to have sexual relations than a selfish and unkind one. That is reward enough, is it not, for most men? Happy marriages mean frequent, enjoyable sexual relations.

GOD'S WEEKLY GIFT

God gave mankind a day of rest in seven. This principle of mandatory rest is built into God's creation (Gen. 2:2). Not surprisingly, then, when God deals with his people in redemption, he continues to mandate one day in seven as a day for resting from work (Ex. 20:8–11). In the New Covenant, the Sabbath is replaced by the Lord's Day: 'I was in the Spirit on the Lord's day' (Rev. 1:10). The one in seven principle remains since it is a creational principle.

God gave this day as a gift to mankind for our good. We are not to first think of our liberties being taken away by this day. Rather, we should thank God that he desires for us and grants to us rest from our worldly employments. Resting is not an option in our contemporary world where the cumulative effects of the 'rat race' are devastating. So, for example, failing to rest is a violation of the sixth commandment, 'You shall not kill.' Burnout, stress, and busyness, are often the result of personal sins. God is not a hard task–master; he remembers that we are dust (Ps. 103:14).

If we follow God's ordained pattern for living, we can expect that his wisdom for our lives will bring blessing. We need rest to function well. We need a day to focus on the Lord, be with his people, and help others. Even those who do not believe that the Sabbath remains in the New Covenant often recognize the wisdom of resting and worshipping on the Lord's day. Some of the best 'Sabbatarians' I know are not Sabbatarians. They acknowledge that slavery to the world is a real threat and one way to avoid such is to pause each week, rest, and enjoy God's gracious provision.

Eugene Peterson says it well: 'If you don't take a Sabbath, something is wrong. You're doing too much, you're being too much in charge. You've got to quit, one day a week, and just watch what God is doing when you're not doing anything.'[32]

 Just because your life may be difficult at a certain time does not necessarily mean you are suffering the consequences for a specific sin in your life (think of the life of Job). But when those times arise, you can use them as opportunities to examine your relationship with God. Is it possible that the hardships you suffer are the result of some unrepented sin?

12

IDEAS FOR GOOD WORKS

The nature of truly good works is not to foster pride. This so—called fear that people have of doing too many good works is not something I have had to address much as a pastor. Pride and hypocrisy are rarely, if ever, a result of someone doing too many good works. They may do works, but these works are not those which qualify as 'good' according to God's word.

The nature of good works keeps us humble. Why? We are amazed that God could reward such imperfection. But we are also brought to the humbling reality that he would use us to accomplish his purposes. Amazing: that the omnipotent, all—wise God would use humans to bring about the salvation of sinners.

The need of the day, as it always has been, is for Christians to seek first the kingdom of God. In doing this there is a promised reward: 'and all these things will be added to you.' Material blessings come to those pursuing God's kingdom as their greatest priority (see Matt. 6:31). But the general principle is what matters in our goal to do good works. The kingdom comes first. Christ's interests are ours. Christ loves, more than anything else in this world, the church. How concerned are we for it, missions, supporting future ministers, or ministering to widows and orphans?

We cannot out-give God. Once we, by faith, for the glory of God, give towards his kingdom, we find that we end up receiving as we give. Amazing! God gives freely and abundantly as we give to him. In the account of the poor widow, we might be inclined to think she went too far only to find Jesus blessing her for her sacrifice (Luke 21:1–4):

> Jesus looked up and saw the rich putting their gifts into the offering box, and he saw a poor widow put in two small copper coins. And he said, 'Truly, I tell you, this poor widow has put in more than all of them. For they all contributed out of their abundance, but she out of her poverty put in all she had to live on.

Are we to think that Jesus did not care about this widow? Did she lose in any way? No and no! Consider Mary's extravagant act in John 12:1–8, which, again, Christ receives in the midst of hypocritical opposition that the money could have been used for the poor. The kingdom comes first, no matter what. And when we put the kingdom first we will find that we cannot ever lose by putting the interests of God and Christ before our own.

YOU WILL BE REPAID AT THE RESURRECTION

The Bible speaks a great deal about helping people in need. True generosity often involves helping those who are unable to help you. Much of our help towards others can be very 'strategic' in the sense that we know they are able to give us something in return. But to help those who can give you very little in return, except perhaps a 'thank you' is a sign of whether we have a generous spirit. This seems to be one of the main points of the parable of the great banquet in Luke 14. At the home of a ruler of the Pharisees, Christ made the following point (Luke 14:12–14):

> When you give a dinner or a banquet, do not invite your friends or your brothers or your relatives or rich neighbors, lest they also invite you in return and you be repaid. But when you give a feast, invite the poor, the crippled, the lame, the blind, and you will be blessed, because they cannot repay you. For you will be repaid at the resurrection of the just.

In the church, there is a natural temptation to gravitate to people appealing both in appearance and social standing. This is quite normal. But the gospel is not 'normal'. The gospel turns our worlds and ideas upside down. We who have are to share with those who do not. In so doing, we are promised that we will be 'repaid at the resurrection of the just' (Luke 14:14). This must not mean we will be repaid with salvation, but with a promised reward.

Of course, our help extends to those outside the church: 'So then, as we have opportunity, let us do good to everyone, and especially to those who are of the household of faith' (Gal. 6:10). So yes, we especially take care of our brothers and sisters in Christ, but not merely them. We let our light shine before men (Matt. 5:16). Indeed, when we do good to others, there is the possibility that God will use our works to bring about salvation: '...let your light shine before others, so that they may see your good works and give glory to your Father who is in heaven' (Matt. 5:16). What an incredible reward to know that we were instruments used by God to bring about the salvation of a sinner once destined for eternal damnation.

13

A TEST

> Then I heard what seemed to be the voice of a great multitude, like the roar of many waters and like the sound of mighty peals of thunder, crying out: Hallelujah! For the Lord our God the Almighty reigns. Let us rejoice and exult and give him the glory, for the marriage of the Lamb has come, and his Bride has made herself ready; it was granted her to clothe herself with fine linen, bright and pure—for the fine linen is the righteous deeds of the saints. (Rev. 19:8).

Here is a test, in light of reading the words above. When you read this passage, do you think of the 'fine linen' as the righteous deeds of Christ imputed to the saints? Some authors make this argument.[33] Beale, however, takes a different view: 'Good works are a noncausal necessary condition' for entering heaven (as he points the readers to Rom. 2:6–8; 2 Cor. 11:2).[34] Specifically, the 'fine linen' in Revelation 19:8 is, according to Beale, 'the reward for (or result of) the righteous deeds of the saints.'[35] His next remarks are:

> Consequently, the saints are clothed with pure linen as a symbol of God's righteous vindication of them because, though they were persecuted, they were righteous on earth. The full meaning of the pure garments is that God's righteous vindication involves judging the enemy, which shows that the saints' faith and works have been right all along. The dual sense of 'pure linen' in 19:8 suits admirably the rhetorical purpose of the entire Apocalypse, which includes exhortations to believers to stop soiling their garments (3:4–5) and not to be 'found naked' (3:18; 16:15). This underscores the aspect of human accountability, which is highlighted by 19:7b: 'his bride has prepared herself.' ... From the human side, the good works focus on the saints' witness to their faith in Christ, which is supported by the focus on witness in v 10 and by the direct linkage in 3:4–5 of white clothing with the notion of witness (cf. likewise 3:14 with 3:18).[36]

Good scholars, theologians, and pastors can sometimes have such an aversion to the dangers of moralism, 'neo-nomianism,' or legalism, that they seem to approach the Scriptures in a way where they see 'imputation' in places where the Scriptures are speaking rather obviously about the habitual righteousness of God's people (cf. Matt. 5:20 as an example).

Beale's position helps prove the argument of this book. A 'justification–centrism' approach to the Scriptures is robbing us of a doctrine of good works and rewards that God intended to be a blessing to his people and not a curse. I think we harm the doctrine of justification by faith alone (whereby our sins are forgiven and Christ's righteousness is imputed to us) when we find this doctrine in places where the Scripture is speaking about sanctification. Opponents of this Reformation doctrine end up finding our case so weak that we have to strain for the doctrine in places we have no business finding the doctrine of justification.

CONCLUSION

Augustine famously said, 'O Lord, command what you will and give what you command.' God commands that we, as his children, do good works. But the God who commanded us to do good works is also the God who prepared in advance these good works for us to do. He is the God who provides us with the strength to do the works he has commanded. More than that, he is the God who rewards us, out of grace, not merit, for our good works.

These good works do not even need to be perfect works like the works of our Savior. His perfect works, leading to his great sacrifice on the cross for our sins, make possible a context whereby God rewards us for our works with rewards far and beyond what our works could ever be worth. Thankfully, God does not deal with us according to strict justice. He deals with us according to grace and so motivates us constantly to do good in order to be rewarded.

FURTHER READING

Francis Turretin, *Institutes of Elenctic Theology*, ed. James T. Dennison Jr., trans. George Musgrave Giger. 3 vols. (Phillipsburg, N.J.: P&R Publishing, 1992), 3:621–630.

Four Views on the Role of Works at the Final Judgment (Counterpoints: Bible and Theology) (Zondervan, 2013).

Richard Gaffin, *By Faith, Not by Sight: Paul and the Order of Salvation* (Phillipsburg, N.J.: P&R Publishing; Second Edition, 2013).

WESTMINSTER CONFESSION OF FAITH

XVI

OF GOOD WORKS

I. Good works are only such as God hath commanded in his holy Word, and not such as, without the warrant thereof, are devised by men out of blind zeal, or upon any pretense of good intention.

II. These good works, done in obedience to God's commandments, are the fruits and evidences of a true and lively faith: and by them believers manifest their thankfulness, strengthen their assurance, edify their brethren, adorn the profession of the gospel, stop the mouths of the adversaries, and glorify God, whose workmanship they are, created in Christ Jesus thereunto, that, having their fruit unto holiness, they may have the end, eternal life.

III. Their ability to do good works is not at all of themselves, but wholly from the Spirit of Christ. And that they may be enabled thereunto, besides the graces they have already received, there is required an actual influence of the same Holy Spirit to work in them to will and to do of his good pleasure; yet are they not hereupon to grow negligent, as if they were not bound to perform any duty unless upon a special motion of the Spirit; but they ought to be diligent in stirring up the grace of God that is in them.

IV. They, who in their obedience, attain to the greatest height which is possible in this life, are so far from being able to supererogate and to do more than God requires, that they fall short of much which in duty they are bound to do.

V. We can not, by our best works, merit pardon of sin, or eternal life, at the hand of God, because of the great disproportion that is between them and the glory to come, and the infinite distance that is between us and God, whom by them we can neither profit, nor satisfy for the debt of our former sins; but when we have done all we can, we have done but our duty, and are unprofitable servants: and because, as they are good, they proceed from his Spirit; and as they are wrought by us, they are defiled and mixed with so much weakness and imperfection that they can not endure the severity of God's judgment.

VI. Yet notwithstanding, the persons of believers being accepted through Christ, their good works also are accepted in him, not as though they were in this life wholly unblamable and unreprovable in God's sight; but that he, looking upon them in his Son, is pleased to accept and reward that which is sincere, although accompanied with many weaknesses and imperfections.

VII. Works done by unregenerate men, although for the matter of them they may be things which God commands, and of good use both to themselves and others; yet, because they proceed not from a heart purified by faith; nor are done in a right manner, according to the Word; nor to a right end, the glory of God; they are therefore sinful and can not please God, or make a man meet to receive grace from God. And yet their neglect of them is more sinful, and displeasing unto God.

ENDNOTES

1 John Owen, *The Works of John Owen*, 16 vols. (repr. London: Banner of Truth, 1965–68), 14:13–14.

2 Thomas Watson, *Body of Divinity* (Edinburgh: Banner of Truth Trust, 1974), 129.

3 J.I. Packer, *Knowing God* (Downers Grove, Ill.: InterVarsity, 1993), 206.

4 Packer, *Knowing God*, 207.

5 Matthew Henry, *A Commentary Upon the Whole Bible*. Volume 5. (London, 1835), 33.

6 Willem J. van Asselt, Michael D. Bell, Gert van den Brink, Rein Ferwerda, *Scholastic Discourse: Johannes Maccovius (1588–1644) on Theological and Philosophical Distinctions and Rules* (Apeldoorn: Instituut voor Reformatieondeerzoek, 2009), 251.

7 Obadiah Sedgwick, *The Bowels of Tender Mercy Sealed in the Everlasting Covenant...* (London, 1661), 460–461.

8 James Fisher, *The Assembly's Shorter Catechism Explained, by Way of Questions and Answer* (Philadelphia, 1831), 31.

9 Anthony Burgess, *Vindiciae Legis: or, A Vindication of the Morall Law and the Covenants, From the Errours of Papists, Arminians, Socinians, and More Especially Antinomians* (London, 1646), 125.

10 Burgess, *Vindiciae Legis*, 126.

11 William Ames, *The Marrow of Sacred Divinity* (London, 1642), 50.

12 John Owen, *Works*, 16 vols. (repr. London: Banner of Truth, 1965–68), 3:168–69.

13 Herman Bavinck, *Reformed Dogmatics: Sin and Salvation in Christ*, trans. John Vriend (Grand Rapids: Baker, 2006), 3:292.

14 D. Martyn Lloyd–Jones, *Studies in the Sermon on the Mount* (Grand Rapids: Eerdmans, 1976), 322.

15 Alexander Whyte, *Lord, Teach Us to Pray: Sermons on Prayer* (Vancouver: Regent College Publishing, 1998), 257.

16 Henry, *A Commentary on The Holy Bible: Matthew to Acts*. Volume 5. (London, 1835), 34.

17 Owen, *Works*, 5:71.

18 Thomas Goodwin, *Works*, 12 vols. (repr. Grand Rapids: Reformation Heritage Books, 2006), 7:181ff.

19 Herman Witsius, *Conciliatory, or Irenical Animadversions, on the Controversies Agitated in Britain, under the unhappy names of Antinomians and Neonomians*, trans. Thomas Bell (Glasgow: W. Lang, 1807), 162.

20 Ibid.

21 Goodwin, *Works*, 7:181.

22 *Theoretico–practica theologia, qua, per singula capita Theologica, pars exegetica, dogmatica, elenchtica & practica, perpetua successione conjugantur*, new ed. (Amsterdam, 1724), 704–5.

23 Owen, *Works*, 3:613–614.

24 Owen, *Works*, 3:614.

25 Owen, *Works*, 3:617.

26 Francis Turretin, *Institutes of Elenctic Theology*, ed. James T. Dennison Jr., trans. George Musgrave Giger (Phillipsburg, N.J.: P&R, 1992), 3:623.

27 Turretin, *Institutes*, 3:625.

28 *De verborgentheid des geloofs eenmaal den heiligen overgelevert, of het kort begryp der ware godsgeleerdheid beleden in de Gereformeerde Kerk* (Rotterdam, 1700), 74–75.

29 Stephen Charnock, *The Works of the Late Rev. Stephen Charnock* (London: Printed for Baynes, 1815), 2:641.

30 Turretin, *Institutes*, 2:681.

31 C.H. Spurgeon, 'A Cheerful Giver is Beloved of God,' A Sermon Delivered on Thursday Evening, August 27, 1868.

32 Joshua Lujan Loveless, 'Eugene Peterson on Being a Real Pastor' *Relevant Magazine*, June 7, 2011, http://www.relevantmagazine.com/next/blog/6-main-slideshow/1262-eugene-peterson-on-being-a-real-pastor.

33 J.V. Fesko, *Justification: Understanding the Classic Reformed Doctrine* (Phillipsburg, N.J.: P&R Publishing, 2008), 327.

34 G.K. Beale, *The Book of Revelation*, The New International Greek Testament Commentary (Grand Rapids: Eerdmans, 2013), 935.

35 Beale, *Revelation*, 938.

36 Beale, *Revelation*, 942.

Christian Focus Publications

Our mission statement –

STAYING FAITHFUL

In dependence upon God we seek to impact the world through literature faithful to His infallible Word, the Bible. Our aim is to ensure that the Lord Jesus Christ is presented as the only hope to obtain forgiveness of sin, live a useful life and look forward to heaven with Him.

Our books are published in four imprints:

CHRISTIAN FOCUS

Popular works including biographies, commentaries, basic doc-trine and Christian living.

CHRISTIAN HERITAGE

Books representing some of the best material from the rich heritage of the church.

MENTOR

Books written at a level suitable for Bible College and seminary students, pastors, and other serious readers. The imprint includes commentaries, doctrinal studies, examination of current issues and church history.

CF4•K

Children's books for quality Bible teaching and for all age groups: Sunday school curriculum, puzzle and activity books; personal and family devotional titles, biographies and inspirational stories – because you are never too young to know Jesus!

Christian Focus Publications Ltd,
Geanies House, Fearn, Ross-shire,
IV20 1TW, Scotland, United Kingdom.
www.christianfocus.com